THE BOYS' WAR

THE · BOYS' · WAR

Confederate and Union Soldiers
Talk About the Civil War

by Jim Murphy

CLARION BOOKS
NEW YORK

Title page photograph: *Unidentified Confederate boy.*

All of the pictures in this book are courtesy of the Library of Congress, with the exception of the following:
Title page photograph: Courtesy of the collection of Tim McCarthy. Page xiv print:
Courtesy of The Bettmann Archive.

Clarion Books
a Houghton Mifflin Company imprint
215 Park Avenue South, New York, NY 10003

Book design by Ronnie Ann Herman
Printed in the USA

Library of Congress Cataloging-in-Publication Data
Murphy, Jim,
The boys' war: Confederate and Union soldiers talk about the Civil War/by Jim Murphy.
p.   cm.   Includes bibliographical references.   Summary: Includes diary entries,
personal letters, and archival photographs to describe the experiences of boys, sixteen years old
or younger, who fought in the Civil War.
ISBN 0-89919-893-7—PA ISBN 0-395-66412-8

1. United States—History—Civil War, 1861–1865—Personal narratives—Juvenile literature.
2. United States—History—Civil War, 1861–1865—Children—Juvenile literature.
3. United States. Army—Recruiting, enlistment, etc.—Civil War, 1861–1865—Juvenile literature.
4. Confederate States of America. Army—Recruiting, enlistment, etc.—Juvenile literature.
[1. United States—History—Civil War, 1861–1865—Personal narratives.
2. United States—History—Civil War, 1861–1865—Children.] I. Title.
E464.M87 1990   973.7′ 15054—dc20   89-23959
                                                                                                           CIP
HOR 10 9 8 7 6 5   AC

This book is dedicated to the memory of ANN TROY—
for her constant support and encouragement,
her attention to detail, and her belief that books
can make a difference.

Contents

THE · BOYS' · WAR

"Then the batteries opened on all sides [of Sumter] as if an army of devils were swooping around it."

The War Begins

On April 12, 1861, thousands of Confederate troops were assembled in the still darkness of early morning, looking out toward the mouth of Charleston Harbor. The object of their attention was a squat brick structure sitting on an island one mile away: Fort Sumter. Inside, Robert Anderson, a major in the Union army, along with sixty-eight soldiers, braced for the attack.

Slowly, darkness lifted and Sumter's shape became more and more distinct. Confederate gunners adjusted the firing angle of their weapons, torches poised near the fuses. At exactly 4:30 A.M., General P. G. T. Beauregard gave the command, and the bombardment—and with it the Civil War—began.

An officer inside Fort Sumter described the war's opening shot: "The eyes of the watchers easily detected and followed the shell as it mounted among the stars, and then descended with ever-increasing velocity, until it landed inside the fort and burst. It was a capital shot. Then the batteries opened on all sides [of Sumter] as if an army of devils were swooping around it."

*

For most of us, the Civil War is an event we meet briefly in our history books, a distant and sometimes dry parade of proclamations, politicians, generals, and battles. But for the soldiers who marched off and fought, the Civil War was all too real and consuming. In the pages that follow, you'll meet and hear a very special brand of Confederate and Union soldier—*boys* sixteen years old and younger.

No one knows exactly how many boys managed to join their side's army. Enlistment procedures were very lax, and record-keeping sloppy and often nonexistent. After the war, an army statistician did manage to do a study of several battalions, matching names with birth certificates when possible. From this he estimated that between 10 and 20 percent of all soldiers were underage when they signed up. That means that anywhere from 250,000 to 420,000 boys may have fought in the Civil War!

We might not know how many boys took part in the war, but we certainly have a clear picture of what they experienced and felt. Almost every soldier sent letters home, and a surprising number kept journals and diaries, wrote memoirs about their adventures or articles and histories of their companies.

Usually, their writing is very simple and will sound choppy to our ears. Their spelling is more creative than accurate. This is because they were uneducated farm boys for the most part, away from home for the first time, and only interested in telling what had happened to them and their friends. Everything seemed to fascinate them, too—the long marches, the people they met along the way, the fighting, the practical jokes they played on one another. Even the making of bread was an event worth noting.

It's true that their writing lacks a historian's ability to focus on the "important issues." But it is this directness and eye for everyday details that make the voices of these boys so fresh and believable and eloquent. And it is their ability to create active, vivid scenes that brings the war, in all its excitement and horror, alive after more than one hundred years.

*

Thirty-four hours and over four thousand shot and shells later, Sumter's forty-foot-high walls were battered and crumbling. Fires consumed portions of the interior and were moving closer to the powder magazine. No one inside the fort had been seriously injured in the bombardment, but the outcome of the fight was inevitable. The battle for Fort Sumter ended with the surrender of Union forces on April 14.

Before leaving the fort, Union troops were allowed a brief flag-lowering ceremony accompanied by a cannon salute of fifty guns. (Oddly enough, a freak accident during this ceremony caused an explosion that killed two men—the first victims of the Civil War.) Then, with banners flying and the drums beating the rhythm to "Yankee Doodle," Anderson's small force marched aboard the steamship *Baltic* and headed for New York. Beauregard's soldiers entered the burning fort triumphantly and raised the Confederate Stars and Bars. Even before the smoke had a chance to clear, the nation—including its boys—was ready to go off to war.

An unidentified Union soldier strikes a well-armed pose for the folks back home.

1

"So I Became a Soldier"

WHEN WORD OF Fort Sumter's fall reached him in Washington, President Abraham Lincoln acted quickly, issuing a call for seventy-five thousand volunteers to put down the insurrection. News of the president's call to arms spread with surprising speed—by telegraph, newspaper headlines, and word of mouth. Thomas Galway was fifteen years old and living in Cleveland, Ohio, when he heard.

"As I was coming from Mass this morning," Galway wrote in his journal, "I saw bulletins posted everywhere announcing the bombardment of Fort Sumter. Large crowds were gathered in front of each bulletin board, people peering over one another's head to catch a bit of the news. All seemed of one mind. Everyone talked of war."

Over in Indiana, fourteen-year-old Theodore Upson was working in the cornfield with his father when a neighbor came by. "William Cory came across the field (he had been to town after the Mail). He was excited and said, 'the Rebs have fired upon and taken Fort Sumpter.' Father got white and couldn't say a word.

"William said, 'The President will soon fix them. He has called for 75,000 men and is going to blocade their ports, and just as soon as those fellows find out that the North means business they will get down off their high horse.' "

Much the same was happening in the South. Newspapers hailed the victory at Sumter and predicted that the North would not risk any sort of military action. Public meetings were held to whip up support for the Confederate government.

T. G. Barker, then just thirteen, was attending a small private school in South Carolina. "We were in class," Barker remembered, "all bent over our books, when Headmaster Hammond entered. He did not knock to announce himself, which was unusual, and he did not speak to our teacher either. This was also unusual. He went instead to the middle of the room and said in a serious voice: 'We have had word this morning. Fort Sumter has surrendered and is now a part of the Confederate States of America.' Then he smiled. A second passed and not a sound. Then, as if shot from a cannon, the class stood as one and cheered Hooray! Hooray!"

The political and social causes of the war were numerous and complex, and still produce arguments among historians. Certainly, the profound cultural differences between the North and South were a factor, as were their opposing views on the issue of states' rights. And there is little doubt that an important element of the split was the institution of slavery. Many in the North saw slavery as evil and wanted it abolished completely. Others would accept slavery if it could be confined to the South or if the South agreed to phase it out over a number of years.

For its part, the South viewed slavery as vital to its economic survival. Agriculture, especially the growing of cotton, was its most important business. Slavery provided the cheap labor needed to bring in crops at a profit. Without slavery, Southerners argued, their entire way of life would crumble and be destroyed.

Intensifying matters was the fact that Southern interests were trying to introduce slavery in the newly settled western regions. Many in the North felt that slavery had to be stopped before it had a chance to spread and take hold in the West. As far as Southerners were concerned, the federal government was nothing more than an interfering bully trying to force its views on them.

The slavery question was not a new one at all. It had been discussed and debated, argued and fumed over for nearly fifty years. Tempers were frayed to the point of exploding, and fights had even taken place on the floor of the Senate. When war actually broke out, it was like a pressure-release valve. At last, the country seemed to sigh with relief, something concrete was finally going to settle the dispute.

A regiment of very young Confederate soldiers drills under the walls of Castle Pinkney, South Carolina, 1861.

The result on both sides was an enthusiastic rush to enlist. Men crowded the recruitment centers in the nearest cities or signed on with locally organized units. Emotions ran so high that everywhere enlistment quotas were being met and surpassed easily. Caught up in all of this were boys.

Generally, boys from the North did not join the army because they felt a burning desire to stamp out slavery. One boy's comment about slavery is fairly typical: "I do not know anything about it, whether it is a good thing or a bad thing," he wrote in a letter, "and when talk gets around to it I say very little." Many joined because they wanted to take the defiant South and "set them straight." But most signed up for a simpler reason—to escape the boring routine of farm life and take part in an exciting adventure.

The same spirit of adventure and glory motivated Southern boys as well. A Mississippi recruit said he had joined "to fight the Yankies—all fun and frolic." But underneath the festive attitude was another, deeply felt reason for serving—to defend their homes from a large invading army. One Southern boy made his feelings clear, "I reather die then be com a Slave to the North."

Each side had recruitment rules that expressly banned boys from joining and fighting. At the start of the war, for instance, the Union held that a recruit had to be at least eighteen years old. In spite of this, a tall fourteen- or fifteen-year-old could easily blend into a crowd of men and slip through in the hurry to form a unit. Those questioned about their age might be able to bluff their way past a wary recruiting sergeant. Anyway, how would a recruiter check on an applicant's facts? The standard forms of identification we have today, such as driver's license, social security number, and credit cards, did not exist back then. There were no computers or telephones, either, so verifying someone's birthday was nearly impossible.

Telegraph operators for the Union army relax during the siege of Petersburg, Virginia.

By far the easiest way for a boy to slip into the army was as a musician, especially as a drummer or bugler. These were considered nonfighting positions, so recruiters often allowed a boy to sign on without worrying about his age. The Union army alone had need of over forty thousand musicians, while an estimated twenty thousand served for the South.

A Union drummer boy in full uniform.

Many boys found it surprisingly simple to enlist for duty that would take them into the thick of the fighting. Thomas Galway did. The day after the surrender of Fort Sumter, Galway visited a nearby armory run by a group called the Cleveland Grays. "But they did not seem to me to be the sort of stuff that soldiers are made of, so I went away." That evening, "I went to the armory of the Hibernian Guards. They seemed to like me, and I liked them. So together with Jim Butler and Jim O'Reilly, I enlisted with them. My name was the first on the company's roll to enlist. I didn't tell them that I was only fifteen. So I became a soldier."

On occasion, a boy would enter with the blessings of one or both parents. Ned Hutter went to join the Confederate army near his home-town in Mississippi. When the recruitment officer asked his age, Ned told him the truth: " 'I am sixteen next June,' I said. . . . The officer ordered me out of line and my father, who was behind me, stepped to the table. 'He can work as steady as any man,' my father explained. 'And he can shoot as straight as any who has been signed today. I am the boy's father.' It must have been the way he said the words . . . [because] the officer handed me the pen and ordered, 'sign here.' "

Such support was rare, however, and most boys had to get in by less honest means. A fifteen-year-old Wisconsin boy, Elisha Stockwell, Jr., was one of them. "We heard there was going to be a war meeting at our little log school house," Stockwell recalled. "I went to the meeting and when they called for volunteers, Harrison Maxon (21), Edgar Houghton (16), and myself, put our names down. . . . My father was there and objected to my going, so they scratched my name out, which humiliated me somewhat. My sister gave me a severe calling down . . . for exposing my ignorance before the public, and called me a little snotty boy, which raised my anger. I told her, 'Never mind, I'll go and show you that I am not the little boy you think I am.' "

Sixteen-year-old Edwin Francis Jennison was a private in a Georgia infantry regiment. He would be killed at Malvern Hill, Virginia, in July 1862.

Elisha's hurt and anger calmed after his sister and mother apologized for what had been said. He even promised not to enlist again if he could attend school that winter. They agreed, and Elisha put aside his zeal to fight the Confederacy.

Unfortunately, Elisha's father had other plans for Elisha's winter. He'd signed up himself and his son to burn charcoal, a tedious, dirty, and backbreaking job. When Elisha learned this, he devised a new plan to enlist. First he told his parents he was going to a dance in town. Then he persuaded a friend's father, a captain in the Union army, to accompany him to a nearby recruitment center.

"The Captain got me in by my lying a little, as I told the recruiting officer I didn't know just how old I was but thought I was eighteen. He didn't measure my height, but called me five feet, five inches high. I wasn't that tall two years later when I re-enlisted, but they let it go, so the records show that as my height."

Elisha went home to gather up some clothes and found his sister in the kitchen preparing dinner. He did not mention anything about fighting for the Union, and after a brief conversation, "I told her I had to go down town. She said, 'Hurry back, for dinner will soon be ready.' But I didn't get back [home] for two years."

A young volunteer from Michigan in the "uniform" he wore from home.

2

✧

Marching Off to War

THE EXCITEMENT OF enlisting was soon replaced by the reality of serving. A sad and ironic truth about the Civil War was that neither side had expected the disagreements to turn into actual fighting. Both were certain that another compromise could be worked out. As a result, neither side had an army in place or the arms or materials to outfit one.

The North was in a slightly better position at the start. It had a strong industrial base from which to produce materials and it had a standing army and arms. The trouble was that it would take almost a full year before its manufacturing plants could retool to supply what the army needed. As for the army itself, it numbered only sixteen thousand when the war began, and many of its officers and soldiers would resign to fight for their Southern states. And while the North did have a sizeable number of cannon and rifles, a surprising proportion of these weapons dated back to the revolutionary war!

Early in the war, recruits often found themselves marching in their street clothes and using wooden guns and swords and even cornstalks for training. A lucky unit might find itself outfitted by the proud citizens of its town. This, however, produced a rainbow of uniform colors and styles on both sides. One regiment called itself the Highlands and proudly marched off to battle wearing kilts. The most outlandish uniforms were patterned after those worn by a celebrated French fighting unit known as the Zouaves and consisted of baggy red breeches, purple blouses, and red fezzes.

The South's economic power lay in its production of cotton and not in manufacturing. When Lincoln ordered a complete blockade of all Southern ports, problems in the South multiplied. No wonder recruiting posters made it very clear that "the volunteers shall furnish their own clothes."

The result was a hodgepodge of colors for both armies. When the two sides gathered during the first months of the fighting, it looked like a hastily assembled circus parade and not two serious armies.

Worse, the variety of uniforms often led to fatal mistakes. With smoke blurring vision and emotions running high, inexperienced troops often fired on anyone wearing the enemy's color. And at least one battle was decided by the color of the uniforms. During the Battle of Bull Run in July 1861, Union artillery was ripping apart the Confederate lines from the top of Henry House Hill. When blue-uniformed soldiers emerged from the right, Union officers took them to be friendly infantry and did not fire on them. The blue-clad arrivals (who were really Confederate troops from Virginia) marched up and routed the Union forces without much opposition.

Deciding on a uniform design and color could be done quickly. But manufacturing uniforms for hundreds of thousands of soldiers would take a great deal of time. Before the war, every soldier had to be measured and the cloth for his uniform cut and sewed by hand. Obviously, outfitting two armies this way would take months and months. To speed things up, manufacturers were given a series of graduated standard measurements for uniforms and shoes, and soon they were mass-producing these items by the thousands. This concept of sizes would be used in the production of civilian clothing after the war.

Even after both sides adopted standardized uniforms, the results were not always completely pleasing. A sixteen-year-old in the Union army provides these details about his first uniform: "my trousers were too long by three or four inches; the shirt was coarse and unpleasant, too large at the neck and too short elsewhere. The cap was an ungainly bag with pasteboard top and leather visor; while the overcoat made me feel like a little nubbin of corn in a large husk. Nothing ever took down my ideas of military pomp quite so low."

A regiment of soldiers from New York in typical uniforms. "The more they serve," an observer wrote, "the less they look like soldiers and the more they resemble day-laborers who have bought second-hand military clothes."

Abel Sheeks, aged sixteen, joined the Confederate side with only the clothes he was wearing when he ran away from his Alabama home. Unfortunately, his shirt and pants were the same blue color used by his enemy. He tells how he came by a proper uniform: "I was not very tall and caps and drawers were in short supply, so they went to the older, bigger men. I did not mind this and was happy with what I had, which was what I had brought from home, until the sergeant came to me and said, 'Do you want to be taken for a d—— Yankee in all that blue?' I did not, so after each fight I would search the field for anyone near my size who did not require use of his equipment. I must confess to feeling very bad doing this, believing the dead should not be disturbed . . . but I had no other course. In just a few weeks my uniform was the equal of anyone's."

Once outfitted, a boy had to learn the business of being a soldier. Since arms and ammunition were scarce, there was not a great deal of target practice for either side. He would have to learn how to handle a gun in the heat of an actual battle. That left only the tedious and tiring exercise of drilling.

Both armies needed soldiers who could be moved quickly and precisely during battle. A long column of marching men might have to be positioned to face an enemy approaching head-on. This could happen in thick woods or at night or even in a downpour. And once positioned, the men might have to be repositioned many times either to defend against attacks from the side or to move to another spot on the battlefield. To avoid chaos, even a retreat was supposed to be orderly.

The only way to get these movements down so they were second nature was by practicing them whenever possible. These boys knew the importance of drilling, but that doesn't mean they liked to spend much time at it. One patriotic boy made his opinion clear: "These daily drills, and regimental and brigade reviews and inspections, though very neces-

Artillerymen of the Confederacy, a number of them very young, practice loading techniques before a battle.

sary and exceedingly useful, are felt by nearly all of us to be a great bore. For after 5 or 6 months of hard marching and fighting, to subside into the quiet and monotony and most tedious irksomeness of [drilling] goes very much against the private soldier."

In truth, the boys handled the marching drills easily. They were young, healthy, lean, and energetic, and found that in marching they were the equals of older soldiers. Their comments are often filled with obvious pride. Elisha Stockwell's entry is typical of those made by boys from both armies: "There were nearly all big men in my company, and one said it was a disgrace to take such little boys as Jim Ferguson and me in the company. But the first hard march we were on I saw him played out and laying beside the road. . . . The big man was reduced to a skeleton with chronic diarrhea and got discharged before his first year's service was out."

New recruits from the Ninety-sixth Pennsylvania Infantry learning drill procedures in a camp just outside Washington, D.C.

If the physical endurance required in marching was easy for these boys, the notion of discipline was not. They were not accustomed to taking orders from strangers. A Union boy had a telling brush with authority: "The first day I went out to drill, getting tired of doing the same things over and over, I said to the drill-sergeant: 'Let's stop this fooling and go over to the grocery.'

"His only reply was addressed to the corporal: 'Corporal, take this man out and drill him like hell.' And the corporal did! I found that suggestions were not well appreciated in the army as in private life. . . . It takes a raw recruit some time to learn that he is not to think or suggest, but obey."

The Southern army seems to have been more disciplined and more relaxed at the same time. When sides were being chosen for the war, the South got most of the experienced officers and soldiers. In addition, the president of the Confederacy, Jefferson Davis, was a former soldier and secretary of war. This put the South months ahead of the North in organization and training, and led to its stunning military successes in the first three years of the war. Even so, one Southern historian has described camp life as "one continuous barbecue."

Drilling was held to a minimum, and the notions of saluting, saying "yes, sir" and "no, sir," and keeping an orderly tent were not strictly enforced. Most likely, the Confederate officers realized they did not need all of that to create an efficient fighting unit. These men were literally going to fight an invading army to save their homes; when a battle came, they would follow orders. In addition, the officers realized that their men were not being properly supplied. Why push troops to further aggravation with excess drilling and military form?

This doesn't mean that some Confederate officers did not try to establish tighter rules. But these attempts often produced more hostility than discipline. A private from Georgia wrote an angry letter home about a new rule that required men to remove their hats when they went to the general's tent: "You know that is one thing I wont do. I would rather see him in hell before I will pull off my hat to any man and tha Jest as well shoot me at the start."

Assembling a uniform and getting used to a modest amount of military discipline were just the start for these boys. They often had to deal with harassment from older soldiers. Being able to outmarch an older soldier helped to a degree, but this was often not enough to stop the abuse. Elisha Stockwell tells how he dealt with just such a problem: "One of the company was known as Curly. He was a big husky man and quite handy with his fists. He said he had to try all recruits to see if they could fight, and proceeded to cuff me around until I got quite enough of that play. I told him I didn't enlist to fight that way, but if he would get his gun and go outside of the camp, we would stand thirty or forty rods apart, and I thought I could convince him that I could shoot as well as he could. He turned it off as a joke and said he guessed I would pass. I never liked him after that, but he never bothered me again."

Much the same happened in the Confederate army, as the soldiers in newly formed units tested each other or tried to "see what these little boys are made of." For the most part, some sort of peace was made. But one letter written by a Confederate officer tells of a different outcome.

An older soldier had begun teasing a newly enlisted boy about his size, the poor fit of his uniform, the way he marched, and so on. "This had gone on several weeks," the officer noted, "and the boy was getting quite mad, and for good reason. Then one afternoon words were exchanged and the boy shouted and ran off. He came back with a cocked pistol and demanded that the older man apologize for all of his insulting statements. The other fired his rifle and the boy went down dead. There was nothing we could do." After describing the chaos that followed and the arrest of the older man, the letter concludes, "He was

There are many young-looking faces in this group shot of the Ninety-third New York Infantry.

the first of our unit to be killed, though we had assumed that death would be the result of an enemy ball. They say he was fifteen."

The period of enlisting, outfitting, and training did not take very long, especially in the opening months of the Civil War. Each side rushed to get troops into the field, even if they were sloppy and inexperienced, before the other could attack. Many units had as little as three weeks of instruction before marching into the fight. And in a few instances, boys went directly from their schoolroom to the battlefield.

What boys on both sides had in common was a patriotic and spirited send-off to battle. "One morning," a boy from a small town in Connecticut wrote, "there was great excitement at the report that we were going

While the Sixty-seventh New York Infantry drills in the background, drummers and buglers practice at the foot of the hill.

to be sent to the front. Many of our schoolmates came in tears to say good-by. Our mothers—God bless them!—brought us something good to eat—pies, cakes, doughnuts, and jellies. One old lady brought her son an umbrella. Finally we were ready to move; our tears were wiped away, our buttons were polished, and our muskets were as bright as emery paper could make them. . . . Handkerchiefs were waved at us from all the houses we passed; we cheered till we were hoarse."

The same sort of emotion sent Confederate boys off to war. A. Mathews was almost fifteen when his hometown unit assembled in the town's main street before leaving. "A large turnout of citizens . . . honored the hour of departure of this company of gallant troopers with their presence. . . . [The captain] addressed the company in a most appropriate and forcible speech. His remarks filled the company with emotions and melted his audience to tears."

With this, the soldiers, men and boys, formed neat, straight columns, two abreast, and marched out of town. No doubt many waved good-bye to their families or shouted to friends. Soon, however, the town and festive noise would give way to the dull thud of boots striking the road. It was probably around this time that they recalled one promise the captain had made in his speech. "We will return as honored soldiers," he had said, "or fill a soldier's grave."

Union infantry marching near Harpers Ferry, West Virginia.

3

"What a Foolish Boy"

"DAY AFTER DAY and night after night did we tramp along the rough and dusty roads," writes sixteen-year-old Confederate soldier John Delhaney, " 'neath the most broiling sun with which the month of August ever afflicted a soldier; thro' rivers and their rocky valleys, over mountains—on, on, scarcely stopping to gather the green corn from the fields to serve us for rations. . . . During these marches the men are sometimes unrecognizable on account of the thick coverings of dust which settle upon the hair, eye-brows and beard, filling likewise the mouth, nose, eyes, and ears."

Boys on both sides soon learned a boring fact about life in the army. Soldiers spend more time marching from one place to another than fighting.

At each town, new units would join the troops until the column stretched for miles with no beginning or end in sight. A messenger might fly past on horseback carrying orders for the officer in charge. The column would halt for a half hour or an hour with no explanation of what was happening up ahead. Then suddenly the order would be shouted up and down the line, the drumbeat would sound, and the troops would be on their way again.

Not that they understood what all of this maneuvering was about. It did not take Elisha Stockwell very long to comment on this with his dry wit: "We didn't know where we were going, as a soldier isn't supposed to know any more than a mule, but has to obey orders."

What the common soldiers did not realize was that the commanders for both sides were engaged in a large-scale chess match in which they were the pieces. The first two commanders of the Union army, Lieutenant General Winfield Scott and then Major General George McClellan, had decided on a defensive war, at least until they could amass, outfit, and train a vast army. Both feared that if Confederate troops were able to capture Washington, D.C., civilians and politicians in the North would become demoralized and abandon the fight. They also hoped that the South would lose energy and give up its quest for independence.

The Confederate commander, General Robert E. Lee, adopted a cautiously offensive plan. He knew the Union army outnumbered his by almost two to one and that it had more supplies. He could never hope to win any head-to-head battle. Instead, he decided to use smaller, fast-moving groups of soldiers and cavalry to strike at Union forces in many places, then wheel around and strike again. By poking at the enemy, he hoped to hold his losses down while buying time to build up his forces. And he, like Scott and McClellan, hoped the other side would abandon the fight.

When boys enlisted in the army, they expected to fight the enemy and settle the dispute very quickly. After all, Lincoln's initial call for enlistments asked for only ninety days of service. But after what seemed like an endless amount of marching and a few hard fought battles, it became clear that neither side was going to surrender easily or quickly.

And once they realized the war would last a long, long time, these boys began to miss the things they had left behind—namely their family and friends.

Homesickness was a common problem and found expression in many forms. Singing was one way to express such feelings. One of the most popular war songs for both sides, called "Tenting Tonight," was written even before the first year of fighting was completed. A few of its lines go:

> We're tenting tonight on the old camp ground,
> Give us a song to cheer our weary hearts,
> A song of home, and the friends we love so dear.
>
> We've been tenting tonight on the old camp ground,
> Thinking of days gone by, of the loved ones at home
> That gave us the hand, and the tear that said "good-bye!"

Many boys simply put down what they felt in their own words. One Southerner, J. B. Lance of Buncombe County, North Carolina, was already tired of life away from home in October 1861. His message was simple and direct, and yet poignant: "Father I have Saw a rite Smart of the world Sence I left home But I have not Saw any place like Buncomb and hendersn yet."

It's easy to see why these boys developed such feelings. They were so young they had little real sense of who they were or how they fit into the world. The one solid and reliable thing they knew—their families—had been left behind. Their futures were uncertain. And they had not had time to develop real friendships with the others in their units. John Delhaney managed to capture in his journal this feeling of being apart and alone: "I felt strange enough, lying down this my first night in camp.

The strange faces and forms, the near and distant sounds of an army of men talking, shouting, singing, and all upon different subjects; the croaking frogs, cries of the Whip-poor-Will, the glare of the camp fires and the neighing of horses and the deep shadows of a dark night overhanging all; all these were not calculated to allay my uneasiness of mind or lighten my heart of its cares."

*

Despite the endless marching and the tactics of avoidance both sides seemed to favor, the war would eventually catch up with these boys. One day, they would hear the dull thudding of large cannons, known as thirty pounders, being fired in the distance. Plumes of smoke would rise from a nearby valley. As they would draw nearer the action, the firecracker sound of small-arms fire grew more and more frequent.

These Union soldiers don't look very military, but their mortar, nicknamed "Dictator," could hurl shells 2½ miles with deadly accuracy.

An officer would call their company to order. Rifles would be loaded and blankets and haversacks piled in a heap against a tree to wait their return. Then they would move off toward the fighting, their eyes searching the mysterious forest around them for the enemy.

It was often well before they had a chance to fire a shot in anger that these boys learned about the cruel horrors of war. Elisha Stockwell's unit was one mile from the fighting at the Battle of Shiloh when he had this experience: "The first dead man we saw was a short distance from the clearing. He was leaning back against a big tree as if asleep, but his intestines were all over his legs and several times their natural size. I didn't look at him the second time as it made me deathly sick. A little farther on we saw lots of dead men scattered through the woods where they had fallen the day before."

The officer would order the men on, not allowing them to dwell on what they were seeing or feeling. Keep low, keep low, he would shout. Stay alert, boys. The enemy is near. Gunfire grows heavy not more than one hundred yards to the left, and yelling can be heard, though the words are unclear.

What follows are the views of five boys going into battle for the first time. While each one fought in a different battle, their voices and experiences form a remarkably unified picture of what fighting must have been like for an inexperienced soldier.

Thomas Galway recounts what happened to his unit as it moved closer to the gunfire: "Before we had gone far we came to a hanging rock with a tree felled across the road under it. Evidently this barricade had been put there for a purpose. As we stepped over the log we said to one another, 'There is something here. We shall soon see what it means.'

"We were scarcely over the log when a sheet of flame burst through from the top of the cliff. The detonation was startling to our unaccustomed ears."

This unidentified Confederate soldier had his leg shattered early in the battle. He wrapped a cotton shirt around the wound and continued fighting until a bullet struck him in the heart.

Soldiers killed at the Battle of Antietam, 1862.

Suddenly, the war that had been a romantic dream was all around them like angry bees. Elisha Stockwell found himself facedown on the ground, shells exploding all around and soldiers screaming for help: "I want to say, as we lay there and the shells were flying over us, my thoughts went back to my home, and I thought what a foolish boy I was to run away and get into such a mess as I was in. I would have been glad to have seen my father coming after me."

But the only things searching for these boys were the shot and shell of their enemy, which ripped up clots of earth, stripped the leaves from the trees, and too often found their mark. Soon a voice can be heard urging the soldiers to get up and move forward. It's an officer from another unit, who actually grabs some soldiers by the shirt, hauls them up, and pushes them into motion. Young Tyler Wise tells about these tense moments. "We moved quite lively as the Rebel bullets did likewise. We had advanced but a short distance when we came to a creek, the bank of which was high, but we slid, and wading through the water to the opposite side and began firing at will. . . .

"For two hours, the contest raged furiously. The creek was running red with precious blood spilt for our country. My bunkmate and I were kneeling side by side when a ball crashed through his brain. With assistance of two others I picked him up, carried him over the bank in our rear and laid him behind a tree." But there was no time to grieve or even feel sorry; a few moments later, Wise reentered the battle.

Naturally, Confederate boys went through much the same initiation. What was different was that Confederate troops seemed to do much better in the early fighting. Credit for this success has to go to the Southern officers. They did a much better job of keeping their men united and pressing forward even in the midst of heavy fire. And they tolerated such unmilitary but emotionally unifying behavior as the dreaded "rebel yell."

No two descriptions of the rebel yell are alike, though one soldier described it as "a mingling of Indian whoop and wolf-howl." Whatever it sounded like, it seems to have worked well for many soldiers. William Chambers described his first experience with it: "I always said if I ever went into charge, I wouldn't holler! But the very first time I fired off my gun I hollered as loud as I could, and I hollered every breath till we stopped."

This Virginia boy, Andrew J. Hoge, was killed at Gettysburg, 1863. It would be over a year before his remains were collected and buried.

Another Confederate soldier describes its use in battle: "Then the Rebel yell was sounded, and right into their ranks we dashed, pouring a deadly volley into their very faces. A moment more and the enemy broke and fled wildly, the scouts keeping in hot pursuit. On they ran, and the rout was complete."

When either side broke ranks in search of safety, the result was a confusion of soldiers racing through forests or across fields. Elisha Stockwell's first fight ended like this: "We had lost all formation, and were rushing down the road like a mob. When we got to the foot of the hill, there was a small stream of water from the rain of the night before. We stopped there and got behind a small tree. I could see the little puffs of smoke at the top of the hill on the other side some forty rods from us, and I shot at those puffs. The brush was so thick I couldn't see the Rebs, but loaded and fired at the smoke until a grape shot came through the tree and knocked me flat as I was putting the cap on my gun. I thought my arm was gone, but I rolled on my right side and looked at my arm and couldn't see anything wrong with it, so got to my feet with gun in my hands and saw the Rebs coming down hill just like we had.

"The road was full for several rods, and I shot for the middle of the [charging] crowd and began loading. But as they were getting so close, I looked behind me to see what the rest [of my friends] were doing. I saw the colors going out of sight over the hill, and only two or three men in sight. As I started to run, I heard several shout, 'Halt!' But I knew it was the Rebs, and I hadn't any thought of obeying them."

Such undisciplined retreats could often cover miles, with soldiers tossing aside their rifles, ammunition, and hats to lighten their loads. Civilians, who often picnicked on nearby mountains to watch Civil War battles, might even find themselves trampled by panicking soldiers. A few soldiers would not stop running until they reached home.

Gradually, the fighting would lessen and then stop. Straggling soldiers would regroup. Night would settle on the battlefield, and the eerie shadows of soldiers could be seen moving across it, searching out the groaning wounded and digging hasty graves for the dead.

Meanwhile, in camp, exhausted soldiers huddled around the fire, ate, and tried to rest up for the next day's fighting. Some would tell tales of their bravery or of some strange thing they had seen during the fighting. Others, like Tyler Wise, would think about the friend they'd lost that day. "I dreamed of my bunkmate last night," Wise wrote in his diary. "Wonder if his remains will be put where they can be found, for I would like, if I ever get the chance, to put a board with his name on it at the head of his grave."

A weary Union camp at Nashville settles down for the night.

The drum corps of the Eighth New York State Militia in June 1861. At this early stage of the war, their uniforms were still light gray.

4

Drumbeats and Bullets

THE GROGGY SOLDIER woke up to a persistent, brain-rattling drumming noise. *Thrump. Thrump. Thrump.* He rolled over in an attempt
to ignore the sound and pulled his blanket up over his head. The
drumming went on and intensified as drummers all over camp signaled
the call to muster. There was no escaping it, and eventually—and usually with a grumble—the soldier got up to start another day.

Soldiers probably came to hate the sound of the drums, especially
when they heard them on a drizzly, cold morning. Yet drummer boys
who served during the Civil War provided valuable service to the armies
of both sides, although some didn't realize it at first.

"I wanted to fight the Rebs," a twelve-year-old boy wrote, "but I was
very small and they would not give me a musket. The next day I went
back and the man behind the desk said I looked as if I could hold a drum
and if I wanted I could join that way. I did, but I was not happy to change
a musket for a stick."

This boy was disappointed at being assigned a "nonfighting" and, to him, dull job. Most likely, he saw himself always drumming in parades or in the safety of camp. He would soon learn differently.

The beat of the drum was one of the most important means of communicating orders to soldiers in the Civil War. Drummers did find themselves in camp sounding the routine calls to muster or meals and providing the beat for marching drills. But more often than not, they were with the troops in the field, not just marching to the site of the battle but in the middle of the fighting. It was the drumbeat that told the soldiers how and when to maneuver as smoke poured over the battlefield. And the sight of a drummer boy showed soldiers where their unit was located, helping to keep them close together.

Drummers were such a vital part of battle communication that they often found themselves the target of enemy fire. "A ball hit my drum and bounced off and I fell over," a Confederate drummer at the Battle of Cedar Creek recalled. "When I got up, another ball tore a hole in the drum and another came so close to my ear that I heard it sing."

The drum corps of the Ninety-third New York Infantry. Samuel Scott (fifth from left) was sixteen when this photo was taken, and Newton Peters (seventh from left) was just fifteen.

Naturally, such killing fire alarmed many drummer boys at first. But like their counterparts with rifles, they soon learned how to face enemy shells without flinching. Fourteen-year-old Orion Howe was struck by several Confederate bullets during the Battle of Vicksburg in 1863. Despite his wounds, he maintained his position and relayed the orders given him. For his bravery, Howe would later receive the Medal of Honor.

Drumming wasn't the only thing these boys did, either. While in camp, they would carry water, rub down horses, gather wood, or cook for the soldiers. There is even evidence that one was a barber for the troops when he wasn't drumming. After a battle, most drummers helped carry wounded soldiers off the field or assisted in burial details. And many drummer boys even got their wish to fight the enemy.

Fighting in the Civil War was particularly bloody. Of the 900 men in the First Maine Heavy Artillery, 635 became casualties *in just seven minutes* of fighting at the Battle of Petersburg. A North Carolina regiment saw 714 of its 800 soldiers killed at Gettysburg. At such a time, these boys put down their drums and took up whatever rifle was handy. One such drummer was Johnny Clem.

Clem ran away from home in 1861 when he was eleven years old. He enlisted, and the Twenty-second Michigan Regiment took him in as their drummer, paying him thirteen dollars a month for his services. Several months later, at the Battle of Shiloh, Clem earned the nickname of "Johnny Shiloh" when a piece of cannon shell bounced off a tree stump and destroyed his drum. When another drum was shattered in battle, Clem found a musket and fought bravely for the rest of the war, becoming a sergeant in the fall of 1863.

The Civil War would be the last time drummer boys would be used in battle. The roar of big cannons and mortars, the rapid firing of thousands of rifles, and the shouts of tens of thousands of men made

Johnny Clem, twelve, just after the Battle of Shiloh, 1862.

hearing a drumbeat difficult. More and more, bugles were being used to pass along orders. Military tactics were changing, too. Improved weapons made it impractical to have precise lines of soldiers face their enemy at close range. Instead, smaller, fast-moving units and trench warfare, neither of which required drummers, became popular.

Even as their role in the fighting was changing, Civil War drummers stayed at their positions signaling orders to the troops. Hundreds were killed and thousands more wounded. "A cannon ball came bouncing across the corn field," a drummer boy recalled, "kicking up dirt and dust each time it struck the earth. Many of the men in our company took shelter behind a stone wall, but I stood where I was and never stopped drumming. An officer came by on horseback and chastised the men, saying 'this boy puts you all to shame. Get up and move forward.' We all began moving across the cornfield. . . . Even when the fighting was at its fiercest and I was frightened, I stood straight and did as I was ordered. . . . I felt I had to be a good example for the others."

A Union drum corps poses in 1862.

Pork, hardtack biscuits, sugar, and coffee being loaded into supply wagons at the Commissary Depot in Cedar Level, Virginia.

5

A Long and Hungry War

ONCE IT WAS CLEAR to both sides that they were in a real fight, one that was not simply going to fade away, some important steps had to be taken. First, many more soldiers would be needed. Second, the ragtag amateur soldiers would have to be better trained. And third, somehow, enough supplies and arms had to be found to keep the soldiers in the field.

The first two needs were reasonably easy to address. Before the first year of fighting was over, both the Union and Confederate governments issued calls for massive numbers of enlistments. These would not be ninety-day enlistments; the new soldiers would be signing on for three years! An estimated 2,898,304 would serve in the Union army during the war, while the Confederate side would see almost 1,500,000 join.

Creating good soldiers began with the officers. Many men had become officers through political favoritism or because they had been able to sign up enough recruits to make a regiment. Others were elected by the soldiers themselves, usually because they were popular, easygoing fellows. Such officers did not know how to handle groups of men during battle and never earned their respect, either.

The Union moved quickly to weed out these weak officers. Military boards were set up to examine officers, and over the next few months hundreds of officers were discharged or resigned. This did not put a complete end to the practice of appointing or electing officers, but it did establish some minimum standards for competence.

As noted before, the South seemed to have gotten a better crop of officers from the start. Why did this happen? One reason is that of the eight military schools the country had in 1860, seven were located in the South. Generally, officers remained loyal to the regions where they were trained. Of the 1,900 men who had attended Virginia Military Academy, over 1,750 would serve for the South. This does not mean that every officer in the Confederate army was a seasoned veteran. One very young officer wrote, "While here at Taylorsville we have daily evening battalion drills, of which I know nothing in the world. In vain do I take Harder's Tactics in hand and try to study out the manoeuvers."

It was not at all unusual to see large formations of soldiers being drilled by an officer with his manual of instructions firmly in hand. But as the officers learned their duties, so did the soldiers.

The one problem neither side quite solved was how to supply their troops with enough food. A few statistics will show the immense size of the problem faced by each side. An army of 100,000 soldiers required 2,500 supply wagons and at least 35,000 horses and mules (for use by the cavalry and to haul the wagons and artillery). Men and horses consumed 600 tons of supplies *every day!*

Food had to be gathered from various growing regions and then shipped hundreds of miles by train to supply bases. Then it had to be loaded into wagons and brought to the troops in the field. As these full wagons were moving in, empty wagons had to be on the way back to the supply depots to load up the next day's supplies. All of this movement had to be timed and carried out with precision if soldiers were going to be fed on time.

After a fumbling first year, both the Union and Confederate armies managed to organize and coordinate their supply efforts. And they worked reasonably well for the most part. Young Thomas Galway

Because supplies were generally scarce, a regiment was allowed a specific amount of each item. Here loaves of bread are weighed before distribution to the troops.

seemed pleased with his rations: "The food issued to the soldiers is very good and in ample quantity. It consists of salt pork or fresh beef; soft bread baked in field ovens, and hard tack on the march and in campaign; coffee and sugar; for vegetables, desiccated potatoes; mixed desiccated vegetables for soup; and beans, rice, and onions. Besides these, we can buy from the sutler all sorts of delicacies such as oysters, canned fruit, cheese, raisins, tobacco, and last though not least, whisky."

But the food-supply system was a delicate ballet of movement that could be disrupted by any one of a number of things. Spring rains might turn the dirt roads into a quagmire of mud that could delay wagons for several days. A sudden movement of troops might put them in an area without adequate roads, cutting them off from supplies for days or weeks. One sixteen-year-old soldier from New York, Charles Nott, tells about his regiment's troubles during a particularly cold winter: "Again we sat down beside [the campfire] for supper. It consisted of hard pilot-bread, raw pork and coffee. The coffee you probably would not recognize in New York. Boiled in an open kettle, and about the color of a brownstone front, it was nevertheless . . . the only warm thing we had.

The cooks are about to serve a hot meal.

The pork was frozen, and the water in the canteens solid ice, so we had to hold them over the fire when we wanted a drink. No one had plates or spoons, knives or forks, cups or saucers. We cut off the frozen pork with our pocket knives, and one tin cup from which each took a drink in turn, served the coffee."

Another common complaint among soldiers was that the food they did get was almost always the same—a never-ending diet of salt pork, dried beef, beans, potatoes, turnips, and corn. After eating army food for nearly three years, Frank Carruth wrote to his sister: "I want Pa to be certain and buy wheat enough to do us plentifully—for if the war closes and I get to come home I never intend to chew any more cornbread."

Luxuries such as eggs, milk, butter, wheat flour, and sugar were scarce at the best of times and often absent for months. No wonder that one boy, R. O. B. Morrow, could write with such enthusiasm about this meal: "We are now permitted to get something to eat. I ran into a store, got hold of a tin wash pan, drew it full of molasses, got a box of good Yankee crackers, sat down on the ground in a vacant lot, dipped the crackers into the molasses, and ate the best meal I ever had."

Stores weren't always handy, especially in wilderness areas. At these times, soldiers could buy things from sutlers. Sutlers were not an official part of the military, but they were permitted to trail after troops and sell things like food, razor blades, paper, and thread. Sutlers acquired these hard-to-come-by items directly from the manufacturers or through European sources. Often, they bought stolen goods and then charged soldiers two or three times the original purchase price. At one point in the war, eggs were selling for six dollars a dozen and bacon cost fifteen dollars a pound!

Sutlers not only charged high prices, sometimes they would refuse to sell food to soldiers they did not know or did not like. Whenever this

Soldiers lined up outside a sutler's tent.

happened, the young soldiers would find other ways to get a meal. Elisha Stockwell took great delight in outwitting one greedy sutler: "[Ed] saw him put a big sweet potato in one of the wagons, and on the way back he got that potato. It was so long he couldn't hide it in his haversack, so he put the haversack on under his coat, and in camp asked me if I could hide it. I said yes, made a hole in the middle of the fire and covered it with ashes and coals, and we waited till all had laid down [to go to sleep]. We dug it out, it was baked fine and we had all we could eat that night and the next morning." How did Stockwell feel about eating stolen food? Apparently, not bad at all. "That was the best as well as the biggest potato I ever saw."

Whether it was in a letter home or a journal, food was probably the most written-about topic. Soldiers were constantly waiting for food supplies to show up or commenting unhappily about their quality, quantity, and variety when they did arrive. At times like this, soldiers often resorted to foraging to supplement their disappointing meals.

Foraging simply meant living off the land around them. At times, they might hunt deer or bear in the nearby forest, or gather nuts and berries. But these activities took a great deal of time, something a marching soldier did not have. Instead, soldiers had to take a more direct approach to finding a meal—they walked up to a farmer's home and offered to buy whatever food was available. If their request was refused, they would take what they wanted, sometimes at gunpoint.

Both armies had strict rules against foraging, and those caught could find themselves in jail for anywhere from a week to a month. But threats of going to jail did not put a halt to foraging. In fact, when guards were set out at night, they were there to keep soldiers *in* camp as much as to watch for an enemy attack. Still, a hungry boy could always find a way through even the tightest security, as John Delhaney makes clear: "Another nightly occupation is to rob bee hives; and not infrequently when the chorus of [religious] hymns is ascending, parties return from a thieving expedition with hats filled with honey comb."

Finding food was a constant challenge for boys in the Civil War even when safely in camp. Imagine what Charles Nott must have felt after his company became lost in enemy territory and ran out of food. After they had wandered aimlessly for several days and barely escaped capture twice, their luck changed. They stumbled across a house in the woods: "No smoke rises from the chimney. We halt; the sergeant enters the open door; comes back and reports it is just what we want—a deserted house."

After finding corn for the horses, Nott did a quick survey of their newly found bounty. In the yard, he saw chickens, cows, sheep, and pigs. Inside the house, they discovered a jar of molasses, a bag of dried peaches, a haunch of smoked venison, and a barrel of black walnuts, as well as coffee beans and cornmeal.

The food was gathered up, and after the horses had eaten, Nott and his friends continued their search for their army. That night they pitched camp and prepared a truly luxurious meal for themselves. He picks up his story: "Pluck the chickens, and cut them up; mix some meal and water, and make corn dodgers, as the Tennessians do. There are the plates to bake on, and we can try baking it in the ashes. But the coffee—everybody looks forward to it—no matter if it is poor and weak. It is always the tired soldier's great restorative, his particular comfort. The chickens must be stewed in pans and roasted on sticks."

Food for the Civil War soldier was always simple, if not downright plain. Few soldiers were skilled cooks, and even those who did know how to prepare food found themselves hampered by a lack of herbs, spices, and other ingredients. A little salt and pepper might be the only things available to put on a meal. Even so, most boys seem to have found great comfort in any meal, no matter how humble. They were able to escape, even if only for an hour or so, from the fighting and death that surrounded them. A meal was a frail link to their recollections of home and family and a better time.

Charles Nott closes his recollections of foraging with these thoughts: "In the course of half an hour we have good coffee. Chicken and corn dodgers come along more slowly, but after a while we sit around the fire to eat them; and everybody declares that he has had enough, and that it is very good."

The camp of the Union army at Cumberland Landing, Virginia.

6

Home Sweet Home

BOYS IN THE Civil War found themselves challenged constantly—by older soldiers, the quest for food, enemy fire, and their longing for home. And as we've seen, they usually found an inventive solution to deal with whatever came their way. The same was true for their efforts to create a home away from home.

Making a physical home was not always easy for soldiers. During warm weather, they spent a great deal of time marching from one field of battle to the next, usually camping for no longer than two or three days. A simple canvas tent that sheltered anywhere from four to ten men was home. But sometimes even a tent was hard to come by. Charles Nott recalls how he and three friends spent a snowy winter night: "We managed to find four blankets, two of them wet and frozen, and a buffalo skin. The snow was scraped away from the windward side of the fire, and the frozen blankets were laid on the ground—a log was rolled up for a wind-break, and the buffalo [skin] spread over the blankets. On this four of us were stretched, and very close and straight we had to lie."

Exposed to the falling snow, Nott and his three buddies covered themselves with the two dry blankets and fell into a sound sleep.

They would have had a perfectly nice night's sleep except for an unexpected problem. The warmth of their bodies plus the heat from the fire began to thaw the hard ground. The wetness from the ground began to seep between the blankets, and soon they could not sleep there anymore. Fortunately, they were clever enough to solve this new problem.

"We bent down a couple of saplings and spread blankets over them, making a little shed. Under this we crept, after piling plenty of wood upon our fire. The soldier's invariable comfort—his pipe—was at hand, and thus we chatted, smoked and dozed till daylight."

Nott was lucky. He was able to find blankets and wood for his fire. Elisha Stockwell found himself without either, one time. Stockwell's company had followed a group of Confederate soldiers across rough terrain for two days. The supply wagons could not keep up with the soldiers' movement, so when they finally turned around to head back to camp, all that they had was what they were carrying. Stockwell picks up his story here: "We marched back toward Corinth in a cold, drizzly rain, and as I didn't have my blankets, I was wet through. I suffered that night as we had only green wood to make a fire. It stopped raining so I got my clothes partly dried. I lay down on the wet ground to sleep, but would get so cold that I would have to get up and hover over the smoky fire. I put in about the most disagreeable night in my life." A few days later, Stockwell developed a fever and fainted while drilling with his company. "I was shaking with the ague—they call it malaria fever nowadays. As long as I was in the army and nearly a year after I got home, I had it every time I caught cold."

Despite the dismal weather, winter was the best time to make a home. Few large-scale battles were planned, which meant that the soldiers of both armies could expect to be camped in one place for several months in a row. When in winter quarters, soldiers rushed to construct solid structures, using trees and branches, barrels, pieces of wrecked wagons, discarded crates, burlap, and even rocks and mud as building materials. Thomas Galway helped construct an impressive winter home in 1863.

"In general each hut is made to accommodate a noncommissioned officer and from eight to twelve enlisted men," Galway remembered. "The walls, which are made of logs, are twelve to twenty feet long, from eight to ten feet wide, and about five feet high. At the middle of each end a forked stick supports a cross piece. Over this is stretched the shelter tents [of all the men] buttoned together. Usually two thicknesses of tents are spread. This roof keeps out rain and snow. The chimneys are sometimes made of sticks piled crosswise upon one another; sometimes and in fact more often, they are of pork barrels from the Commissary."

Winter camp for the Eighteenth Pennsylvania Cavalry at Brandy Station, Virginia.

Furnishings inside were plain and functional. Barrels could be used to store food or, when empty, turned upside down to serve as tables or chairs. There wasn't enough room for beds or large tables, and the bathroom was a hole dug in the ground several yards from the shelter. Galway does record one bit of decoration: "The walls are covered with illustrated papers and with pictures cut from them. What are most sought after for this purpose are the colored fashion plates in the ladies' magazines. As hardly any women are ever seen, the images of attractive women are put where the boys can feast their eyes upon them."

While Galway and his friends were able to build a solid and some-what cozy winter structure, most shelters were crudely constructed, extremely cramped, and drafty. There are numerous accounts of shelters collapsing under the burden of heavy snow or blown apart by strong gusts of wind. This happened most often to Confederate soldiers in the South, where supplies were short.

John Delhaney and two of his friends were only able to build a shack six feet long and five feet wide before snow and ice made further improvements impossible. Delhaney tells about the cramped sleeping conditions: "We have but four blankets between us, so we must manage economically. The way we adopt is for all three to sleep together, lying on one blanket and covering with the other three. This arrangement is all very well with respect to the length of the blankets, but the width is another matter. Provided we all lie in the same position the blankets cover us snugly enough; but if one takes a different position from the other two, the blankets fail to accommodate all." How did they solve this chilly problem? Delhaney continues his story: "We make the following agreement: We shall all go to sleep in the same position and if during the night one wishes to turn over, he must not do so without giving previous warning. So now when some one of us awakes and wishes for a 'change of base', he wakes up the others and announces his purpose. Thereupon the man in the middle gives the command 'right' or 'left turn', and the movement is made promptly and without disorder."

Camp life with all of its comforts and discomforts created a lasting bond between soldiers. In a real way, this shared experience made the others in each soldier's company both his family and his friends.

When a soldier wasn't being drilled or on guard duty, his time was pretty much his own to do with what he pleased. Many would sleep the day away, or read the latest books and illustrated magazines sent from home. Others would play checkers, write letters home, search for food, or gather in small groups to sing. The most popular pastime seems to have been gambling.

Card playing was the most common form of gambling, but Civil War

Union soldiers relaxing in the field. Some are reading letters from home, while others study newspapers, chat, smoke their pipes, or play checkers. And, of course, card playing was a favorite way to pass time.

soldiers were quick to invent other schemes for betting. For a nickel, a soldier could buy a raffle ticket. If his ticket was drawn from a hat, he might win a cash prize of five dollars or a watch or maybe even a chicken.

Racing was also a favorite pastime. Horse races would bring out hundreds of soldiers to wager on and cheer for their favorite; footraces between companies were just as popular and noisy. But horses and men weren't the only things capable of racing. One company painted a round racecourse on a piece of tent canvas and then had louse races on it.

Gambling was so common in camp that new recruits were often shocked by it. One boy, J. E. Hall, wrote to his father in July of 1861 that "a young man cannot guard himself too closely in camp . . . where to be considered an accomplished gentleman it is necessary to be a scientific and successful gambler."

To counter the bad influences of camp life, ministers and priests often wandered among the men, reading from the Bible and urging listeners to repent of their sins. This practice was especially common in the Confederacy, where the "Great Revival" swept over the army in the opening months of 1863. A minister from that time estimated that over 150,000 soldiers "got religion" that year. One young Confederate soldier named Benjamin Jones wrote to a friend about it: "I hear that a great religious spirit and revival is spreading throughout Lee's army, and there are evidences of it here, and in other camps about Richmond. . . . Many of the openly sinful are growing more temperate and reverent in their conversation and regard for religious things. There is less cursing and profligacy, and much less of card playing in our Company."

John Delhaney also commented on this new religious spirit: "The ministers of the different regiments are now on the alert, and prayer meetings and preaching are beginning to be quite common. Every evening before dusk the chaplains begin preaching, and for miles around you might hear thousands of voices singing hymns."

A priest says mass for the Sixty-ninth New York State Militia in 1861.

When the preachers came around, most soldiers put aside their cards and joined in the service out of respect. But after a while, the initial fervor began to wane and many soldiers grew impatient with the ceaseless lecturing. In time, soldiers began drifting back to their old ways. Ruffin Thomson, in shock, wrote to his mother: "Yesterday was Sunday and I sat at my fire and saw preachers holding forth about thirty steps off, and between them and me were two games of poker, where each one was trying to fill their pockets at the expense of his neighbor."

Money was a preoccupation of all Civil War soldiers. Most of these boys came from very poor families where five dollars was considered a great deal of money. Gambling gave them a chance to make that much money and more with little physical effort. In addition, money was needed to buy supplies not provided by the army from sutlers or stores. Of course, whenever an army arrived in an area, the price of everything shot up. This intensified the need for cash and heightened the lengths to which soldiers would go to "earn" it. Elisha Stockwell stumbled upon a lucrative business when he was camped in the South.

Stockwell and another boy his age discovered that they could buy one dollar of Confederate money from Union soldiers for three cents and then sell it to Southern citizens in town for ten cents. In just one day, he and his new business partner earned almost forty dollars! But then they got greedy: "We bought some of a Wisconsin boy that was printed on white paper. It was just imitation of Reb's money, but wasn't signed. We colored the paper with coffee and got Nate Clapp of my company, who was a good penman, to sign it. We had a genuine bill for a sample, and it passed all right. But the Reb citizen we sold it to found out it was counterfeit, and wouldn't buy any more from the Yanks. So we ruined our business by being dishonest."

Civil War soldiers also loved practical jokes. They would poke fun at each other, at passing civilians, and even at an officer if the mood struck them. Even during the height of the religious movement, a good practical joke was always appreciated. In the same letter in which he mentioned the "great religious spirit," Benjamin Jones devoted a great deal of space to what he referred to as "one of the little comedies": "As a few of the tents had been fixed up with rude dirt chimneys for fireplaces, and Sergeant Pond's was one of these, it gave the boys a fine chance to play their game. And so, one night, one of the smallest among the men, with a bucket of water in hand, was lifted up by a big, strong fellow to the top of the little stick chimney. And just as the choir rang out the alarm [by singing] 'Scotland's burning! Cast on water!' the little fellow on the chimney cast his bucket of water down upon the fire inside, which deluged the whole fireplace, put out the fire, and scattered the embers in every direction. Of course, too, it put a stop to the song, and sent the men quickly out of the tent after the offenders. But not in time to discover who they were."

This sense of fun even applied to the enemy from time to time. One of the true oddities of the Civil War was the amount of fraternization that went on between Union and Confederate soldiers. It makes perfect sense, however, when you consider that they all spoke the same language, held similar religious beliefs, and were raised with the same historical heroes. Elisha Stockwell recalled what happened in 1863 after a failed attempt to storm Confederate fortifications outside of Vicksburg: "After this we dug up to them. It was two rods from the outside of our fort to the outside of the Rebs' fort. Moonlight nights they used to agree to have a talk, and both sides would get up on the breastworks and blackguard each other and laugh and sing songs for an hour at a time, then get down and commence shooting again."

Thatcher Riis was also at Vicksburg and remembered this remarkable scene: "Here a group of four played cards—two Yanks and two Rebs. There, others were jumping, while everywhere blue and gray mingled in conversation over the scenes which had transpired since our visit to the neighborhood.

"I talked with a very sensible rebel, who said he was satisfied we should not only take Vicksburg but drive the forces of the south all over their territory, at last compelling them to surrender. Still, he said, he had gone into the fight, and was resolved not to back out."

More than conversation was exchanged at these times, as Riis makes clear: "From remarks of some of the rebels, I judged that their supply of provisions was getting low, and that they had no source from which to draw more. We gave them from our own rations some fat meat, crackers, coffee, and so forth."

Such contacts undercut some of the animosity and bitterness between the armies. The enemy, it turned out, was human after all, and could be kind and generous as well. Fraternization did not stop the fighting, but it did lead Civil War soldiers to respect their opponents and may have contributed to the remarkable lack of revenge sought at the end of the war.

Telegraph operators resting after the Battle of Gettysburg.

Most of the free time a soldier had was spent with small groups of his friends huddled around the fire. John Delhaney paints a vivid picture of what his company did on a typical night: "After the evening repast they lie around the blazing log and talk of their various campaigns, or perhaps speak of their loved ones at home, wonder how long it will be before they will greet them again, and then they may grow silent and gaze into the glowing embers of the fire, and picture to themselves the forms of early years, the shapes and scenes of bygone days, build castles in the flames and sigh and long for the time when war's loud roar shall cease and peace again pervade their homes."

The fire's flame would die down, and the men would wander back to their tents or huts to sleep. Camp life had its pleasant, peaceful moments, but inevitably the sun would rise to warm the countryside and the fighting would begin again.

A fourteen-year-old Confederate soldier killed by bayonet at Fort Mahone.

7

$\diamond$

Changes

FIGHTING IN A war changes any soldier, but it especially changed the boys who fought in the Civil War. When they had enlisted, they were naive, undisciplined, and used to doing farm-related chores. Given several months of drilling and experience in battle, these boys had turned into true soldiers. Granted, they would never have the spit and polish to impress anyone while on parade, but their skill in the field had been honed to a killing edge.

The fear and confusion that often gripped them in the early fighting gave way to a cooler, more analytical head. In the smoke and roar and chaos of battle, these boys would now hold their lines, obey drum commands, and listen for orders. And when a command was issued, they had learned to follow it even in the face of enemy fire. What follows are several descriptions of later battles that give some idea of what this fighting might have been like.

John Delhaney and his regiment had been positioned on a slight rise of the land near a cornfield when he spotted Union forces moving closer: "In the field below us the enemy are slowly but cautiously approaching, crouching low as they advance behind the undulating tracks in the rich meadows through which they are passing. From the numbers of their flags which are distinctly visible above the rising ground we judge them to be at least two thousand in number."

The Confederate artillery opens fire, and this halts the charge for a while. Then the Union cannons return the fire, destroying all of the Confederate cannons and sending the troops into action again. Delhaney picks up his story: "The Yankees, finding no batteries opposing them, approach closer and closer, cowering down as near to the ground as possible, while we keep up a pretty warm fire by file upon them as they advance. Now they are at the last elevation of rising ground [when] they rise up and make a charge for our fence."

Thomas Galway did not fight against Delhaney, but his description of another battle gives a good idea of what such a fight must have been like from his point of view: "Forward we go over fences and through an apple orchard. Now we are close to the enemy. They rise up in the sunken lane and pour deadly fire into us. Our men drop in every few files. The ground on which we are charging has no depression, no shelter of any kind. There is nothing to do but advance or break into a rout. We know there is no support behind us on this side of the creek. So we go forward on the run, heads downward as if under a pelting rain."

At this point in the charge, reinforcements arrive to support the Confederate lines, and the gunfire intensifies. Galway and his friends are forced to halt and wait for orders: "The fight goes on with unabated fury. The air is alive with the concussion of all sorts of explosions. We are kneeling in the soft grass and I notice for a long time that almost every blade of grass is moving. For some time I supposed that this is caused by the merry crickets; and it is not until I made a remark to that effect to one of our boys near me and notice him laugh, that I know it is bullets that are falling thickly around us!"

Union soldiers camped just outside Chattanooga. This group would be cut off from supplies for weeks and face starvation.

The enemy moves some cannons into place and looses a terrible volley of shot and shell. Galway details its effect: "Lieutenant Delaney is shot. . . . Lieutenant Lantry, poor fellow, is annihilated instantly, near me. The top of his head is taken off by a shell. Our company is narrowing more and more. There is but a small group of us left. Fairchild is bleeding; Campion falls, mortally wounded; Jim Gallagher's head is badly grazed and he rolls, coiled in a lump, down into a ditch."

In the opening months of the war, the tendency would have been for one or the other side to pull troops back to safer locations. Better to yield ground than to give up lives needlessly. But as the war dragged on, pressure mounted from the citizens and politicians back home for some sort of resolution to the conflict. This pressure was passed along to the commanding officers of both armies, resulting in longer and fiercer battles.

Confederate sharpshooter killed at Gettysburg.

At this point in our imagined battle, the Confederate officers see that the Union forces are badly shot up and wavering. This is their chance to strike at the Union line and possibly send it into retreat. Despite their own high casualties, a Confederate charge is ordered and John Delhaney and his fellow soldiers obey instantly: "Now we are over a fence and the [line] we are to charge is right ahead. Again we form in a line and now dashing thro' a cornfield; the bullets whistle thro' the leaves and ears and send many a brave comrade to his last account. But we have no time to think; such is the excitement, such the feeling with which I am inspired that I rush on with the rest, completely bewildered and scarcely heeding what takes place around."

Just seconds before the Confederate charge is launched, the Union officers realize they will be wiped out if they do not act. Galway relates what happened then: "Our ammunition is running low. The order is passed along the line for us to charge. There are no bugles to sound it, but we look at one another and, fixing our bayonets, we raise a cheer and go forward. . . . It is but a hop, skip, and a jump to their lines. Horrible sight! The dead lay piled through this lane, covered with blood."

Such close-range, fierce fighting became more and more common. And because soldiers were more skilled than at the war's beginning, the number of deaths increased dramatically. During the first twelve months of the Civil War, a total of 7,000 Union and Confederate soldiers were killed. The next *two* months alone saw a frightening escalation of the fighting—with over 10,000 more soldiers killed! In the end, over 620,000 soldiers (360,000 Union and 260,000 Confederate) would die, more than the combined total of deaths in all the other wars America has fought in before or since.

The boys fighting in the war were surrounded by its carnage. In the Battle of Gettysburg alone, over 7,000 men would die and another

44,000 would be left wounded or missing in action. Even when not fighting, boys were often confronted by scenes such as this one witnessed by Thomas Galway: "We passed over the old battlefield of Manassas. The rains of two years have uncovered many of the shallow graves. Bony knees, long toes, and grinning skulls are to be seen in all directions. In one place I saw a man's boot protruding from the grave; the stitches had rotted and the sole of the shoe warped downwards while the upper had curled upward, leaving the skeleton toes pointing to a land where there is no war."

A dead Confederate soldier.

Just a few of the dead left on the field at Gettysburg.

Living every day with so much death and mutilation took a profound emotional toll on these boys. Where it might have stunned them before, made them physically ill, and stirred longings for the safety of home, now they turned off those feelings. They rarely dwelt on encounters with death for long and instead ignored them in order to get on with other things. Galway ends his journey through the Manassas battlefield with, "Horrid sights are, to an old soldier, horrid no longer. Toward evening we bivouacked near Gainesville."

It isn't hard to imagine why they acted like this. They had joined the army with friends and neighbors and through shared experiences created a new "family." But as they were becoming a more unified group, the war was slowly eating away at their numbers. Elisha Stockwell had

A burial detail gathers up what is left of the dead at Cold Harbor, Virginia, 1865.

marched off with thirty-two others from his town; two years later only three of them were still alive. One boy who had taken part in several major battles recalled waking just before the Battle of Antietam: "We are aroused early on the 16th by a shell which exploded over the regimental colors, killing Corporal Farmer, the color bearer. A piece of the shell literally cut him in two. But we cooked our breakfast and chatted as usual. Some of the men even gambled."

Such descriptions seem distant and cold to us. How could anyone witness such a horrible scene and go on to eat breakfast so casually! It's important to remember that these boys really were skilled soldiers. They knew that the chance to eat a meal might not come along again soon, especially if the battle turned out to be a large one. And they also knew that to think too much about this aspect of war might distract them and make them less precise and poised in battle.

Still, a sense of sadness creeps into their writing. They knew that they were no longer the innocent boys who had signed up for a great adventure. Private Henry Graves expressed his confusion in this letter home: "I saw the body of a man killed the previous day this morning and a horrible sight it was. Such sights do not effect me as they once did. I can not describe the change nor do I know when it took effect, yet I know that there is a change for I look on the carcass of a man with pretty much such feeling as I would do were it a horse or hog."

As troops assemble to march into battle, an ambulance crew prepares for its day's work.

8

$\diamond$

Prison Bars and the Surgeon's Saw

IN ORDER TO BE efficient fighters, boys in the Civil War had to put their normal fears and worries aside. This does not mean they lost all of their emotions. Far from it. These boys worried about a great deal—where their next meal would come from, the abilities and courage of the officers directly in charge of them, or how to get a good pair of shoes, to name just a few. But there were several specific concerns that were shared by all young soldiers on both sides.

One was a fear of being lost among the great crowds in which they marched and fought and died. It was not uncommon for an army of fifty or one hundred thousand men to look across a battlefield at an equal number of the enemy. This was nothing at all like home, where everybody knew the boys' names and faces. Here a boy was just another body, no more important than the person next to him. There are many accounts of boys, separated from their companies while either marching or fighting, who spent days and weeks trying to find a familiar face.

The biggest fear, however, was of being killed, and of not having their bodies identified properly. This was not as odd a fear as it might seem. After a major engagement, the battlefield would be a confusing, chaotic mess. The ground would be pockmarked with hundreds of craters, the result of the ceaseless cannon and mortar fire. Bits and pieces of shattered trees, cannons, and wagons would litter the earth, while the black smoke of burning buildings and fields created a murky and choking haze. Frightened and wounded horses galloped over the landscape; injured soldiers screamed for water or medical attention. A few wounded soldiers might be seen stumbling to find help, their shirts and pants saturated with blood, some still clinging to a severed arm.

What seeing such a scene must have felt like was captured by young Fred Grant, who had accompanied his father, Lieutenant General Ulysses S. Grant, during the siege of Vicksburg: "The horrors of a battlefield were brought vividly before me. I joined a detachment which was collecting the dead for burial. Sickening at the sights, I made my way with another detachment, which was gathering the wounded, to a log house which had been appropriated for a hospital. Here the scenes were so terrible that I became faint, and making my way to a tree, sat down, the most woebegone twelve-year-old in America."

The minute the shooting stopped, the men who had just fought in the battle went hunting among the churned-up landscape for their comrades, living and dead. Thomas Galway did this after the Battle of Gettysburg: "As for us, we have been attending our wounded and have been picking up such of our dead as we could recognize. Each regiment selects a suitable place for its dead and puts a head-board on each individual grave."

They attended to this chore with as much care as they could muster. They would, after all, want the same attention paid to their remains. But it must have been nearly impossible for the exhausted soldiers. For instance, when Grant's army drove toward Richmond in the spring of

1864, it suffered more than 61,000 casualties. Confederate records have not been preserved, but the South must have had similar losses. The dead who could not be identified, as well as all of the enemy dead, were consigned to a mass, unmarked grave, as Galway makes clear: "The unrecognized dead are left to the last, to be buried in long trenches. . . .

A crowded Union cemetery at City Point, Virginia. Only the graves in the background have markers to identify the dead soldiers and their regiments.

The corpses are brought into rows and counted, the Confederate and Federals being separated into different rows. At the feet of each row of fifty or a hundred dead, a trench is dug about seven or eight feet wide and about three feet deep—for there is not time for a normal grave depth. Then the bodies, which are as black as ink and bloated from exposure to the sun, are placed in the shallow ditch and quickly covered with dirt."

Thousands of soldiers would die alone and be buried without proper religious services and in shallow graves. No one would ever know how they died and no one would ever be able to visit their place of burial. They would be lost forever. No wonder that Confederate soldier E. D.

A nameless grave at the base of a tree at Antietam.

Patterson worried more about home than about the wounds he suffered: "I thought of home far away. . . . I wondered if my fate would ever be known to them. I had a horror of dying alone. . . . I was afraid that none of my regiment would ever find me, and that with the unknown dead who lay scattered around me I would be buried in one common ground. The thought was terrible. How I longed for day. Just that some one would see me die."

To die alone was something every young soldier feared. Yet those who managed to survive battle, but were taken prisoner or wounded, might have preferred that fate to the one that awaited them. For if aspects of the fighting represented a shift to modern warfare, the treatment of prisoners and the sick and wounded was something directly out of the Dark Ages.

While anger and embarrassment at being captured may have helped these boys add drama to their accounts, their suffering was real. "Colonel Davis calls it the Black Hole of Calcutta," John Delhaney said of Fort Henry, the prison he was taken to after being captured at Gettysburg. "Our settling down consists in spreading our blankets on the filthy floor, and although many of us are wounded severely enough to merit beds, but one or two are given even bunks, and these are glad enough to leave them to their former occupants—the vermin."

Supplies of all kinds were lacking, and many boys report having to get their blankets and clothes from the bodies of dead men. Food, always a concern of the soldier, was in even shorter supply. Union soldiers voiced the same complaints about their prison conditions. One boy managed to scratch out a fast description of one of his meals: "Rations at last; one course meal cracker and a small bit of bacon: one ration. We are informed that these rations were issued in advance for the following twenty-four hours. Useless to protest; we had but one remaining right—the right to submit. 'That's the best we can do; we are short of rations for our own troops,' said the major. Most of us devoured the 'twenty-four hours rations in advance' at one standing."

These wretched conditions were made even more horrid by over-crowding. The worst Union prison camp was in Elmira New York, and contained ninety-six hundred prisoners inside a forty-acre enclosure. The Southern prison at Andersonville, Georgia, is considered the most fiendish. It was a sixteen-acre stockade camp designed to hold ten thousand prisoners. But by August of 1864, more than thirty-three thousand had been crammed within its walls without any shelter from the hot summer sun.

Elmira Prison camp in 1864, after tents were replaced by permanent structures.

A view of the crowded Andersonville stockade in Georgia.

A Confederate boy visited the Andersonville prison and came away with these thoughts: "The prison struck me as being at best but a miserable makeshift. The day I saw them they were a sweltering mass of humanity, each unit of which was confined to a space of not more than twenty feet. This of itself—the crowding of thirty-two thousand human beings so thickly together—was sufficient to make the prison unsanitary. But that was not all. I saw whole carcasses of slaughtered animals being cut up and made ready for distribution. The refuse which fell into the creek, together with the filth that washed into it from the hillside during heavy rains, necessarily contaminated the water. . . . I venture to say that on the day I was at Andersonville fully a thousand were in the hospital, and that nearly as many more were sick in the stockade. . . . I don't know exactly how many died that day, but in all probability a hundred at least; for according to the hospital records, the average daily death rate for the month of August, 1864, was fully that number."

The conditions at Andersonville were so bad that it became a death camp. Of the forty-five thousand Union soldiers who were imprisoned there, over thirteen thousand would die of sickness, malnutrition, or exposure. After the war, the commandant of Andersonville, Henry Wirz, would be tried and executed for war crimes—the only such trial to result from the Civil War.

How did these boys manage to survive the ordeal of imprisonment? No doubt their strong, young bodies helped them endure the heat or cold. Many used their imaginations and skills. After telling about the lack of food and water at his prison, Point Lookout in Maryland, one Southern boy noted: "The prisoners carried on all kinds of business. Some made finger rings and breastpins out of gutta purcha [a rubberlike substance made from tree sap], toothpicks and trinkets of different kinds of old bones. I myself was engaged in making crude jewelry, from the proceeds of which I was enabled to purchase many luxuries, such as corn meal, coffee, sugar and tobacco. We found ready sale for such stuff, principally among sympathizers on the outside."

Many took a more direct approach to getting more food, as this Union boy's diary entry makes clear: "Sept. 13th, 1863. Rats are found to be very good for food, and every night many are captured and slain. So pressing is the want of food that nearly all who can have gone into the rat business, either selling these horrid animals or killing them and eating them. There are numbers in the drains and under the houses and they are so tame that they hardly think it worth while to get out of our way when we meet them."

No doubt most of a prisoner's time was spent searching for food and clean water, or trying to make himself comfortable. Despite these struggles, many tell of evenings filled with the singing of popular songs or religious hymns. "Another source of recreation," one boy mentions, "is a quiet promenade during the cool hours of evening. Then you may see

Prisoners at Belle Plain line up to get rations from supply wagons.

hundreds of promenaders passing up and down the prison enclosure in quiet, pleasant, but melancholy converse."

Activity in prison was low-key and energy-saving. But John Delhaney did note one intriguing game that seemed to have captured the fancy of many of his fellow prisoners: "The prisoners nearly every evening are engaged in a game they call 'base-ball,' which notwithstanding the heat they prosecute with persevering energy. I don't understand the game, as there is a great deal of running and little apparent gain, but those who play it get very excited over it, and it appears to be fine exercise."

While life in prison must have seemed like a living hell to those who were captured, the worst fate was for the wounded and sick. The weapons used in the Civil War had ten times the killing power of those used in the Revolutionary War. Flesh was ripped and eyes punctured by flying pieces of metal, cannon shells severed arms and legs with ease, and, because metal helmets were not yet worn, head injuries were very common. Unfortunately, the doctor's ability to treat these wounds or simply to lessen pain was primitive at best.

The science of doctoring was still in its infancy when the Civil War started. Morphine and chloroform were used to ease pain, and when these ran short, whiskey and bourbon had to do. Iron pokers were heated until they were white-hot and then applied directly to wounds to stop the bleeding. And if a wound to an arm or leg seemed too severe or became infected, the usual course of action was to cut off the limb.

After one battle, Elisha Stockwell came upon this scene: "We moved on to the east side of town where they were fetching the wounded. They were laying them in rows with just room to walk between. They had tents for those that were the worst off, and where they were amputating arms and legs. There was a wash-out back of one tent that had a wagon load of arms and legs. The legs had the shoes and stockings on them."

Even minor wounds might end up with what we might consider very drastic treatment. While imprisoned, John Delhaney happened to meet a Union army surgeon: "He is a very fine looking man and has his hand in a sling, for yesterday when operating upon a gangrened wound, the knife with which he was operating cut his finger slightly; and [fearing infection] he very sensibly had his own finger immediately amputated."

Most soldiers looked upon the doctor's work as useless mutilation heaped on top of injury, and the fact that large numbers of the injured would linger in agonizing pain for days only to die did not enhance the reputation of the medical profession. One boy, obviously very angry,

Some of the wounded at Marye's Heights waiting to be transported to the hospital.

wrote a blunt condemnation of what he was witnessing: "I believe the Doctors kills more than they cour. Doctors haint Got half Sence."

Unless absolutely necessary, most soldiers would stay as far away from the doctors as possible and treat themselves as best as they could. Teas made from the bark of slippery elm, willow, and dogwood trees were favored remedies for anything from a cold to infected wounds. Wounds were treated by daily cleaning and the removal of anything foreign.

"Today," wrote a young soldier with several wounds to his leg and back, "Sheppard who is most kind in his attentions to my wounds extracts therefrom 4 maggots and cleanses the wounds thoroughly. They

A busy Union field hospital at Savage Station, Virginia, 1862.

are doing very well now; I mean my wounds." One week later he writes, "Sheppard extracts from my wound several pieces of my pantaloons that had been carried into my leg by the bullet and which worked themselves back to the surface today, taking twenty-two days to go a distance of about 2 inches." All of this was done without any sort of painkiller or antiseptic. Surprisingly, this boy recovered from his wounds.

While bullets and shells accounted for tens of thousands of injuries, more Civil War soldiers were felled by sickness and disease. The sanitary conditions of the camps and prisons were deplorable; drinking water and food were often contaminated. In addition, this was the first time these men had lived in such large groups, which facilitated the spread of fever. Dysentery and diarrhea were the most common diseases. But malaria, pneumonia, bronchitis, and scurvy were also common.

Oddly, measles, a disease we consider relatively harmless, turned out to be a major problem for boys in the Civil War. Once the disease took hold, it could sweep through a camp in a matter of days. One gathering of ten thousand new recruits was hit by measles, and before the week was out, more than four thousand had contracted the disease. The disease was so common that it became standard procedure to withhold new troops from active duty until they were "put through the measles."

The treatment for all of these diseases was bed rest and plenty of liquids. Even so, one statistician estimates that more than half of all the deaths in the Civil War were caused by fevers! A boy, J. W. Love, may have summed up the situation perfectly in his letter home: "T. G. Freman is Ded and they is Several mor that is Dangerous with the fever. They hev been 11 Died with the fever in Co. A since we left hinston and 2 died that was wounded so you now See that these Big Battles is not as Bad as the fever."

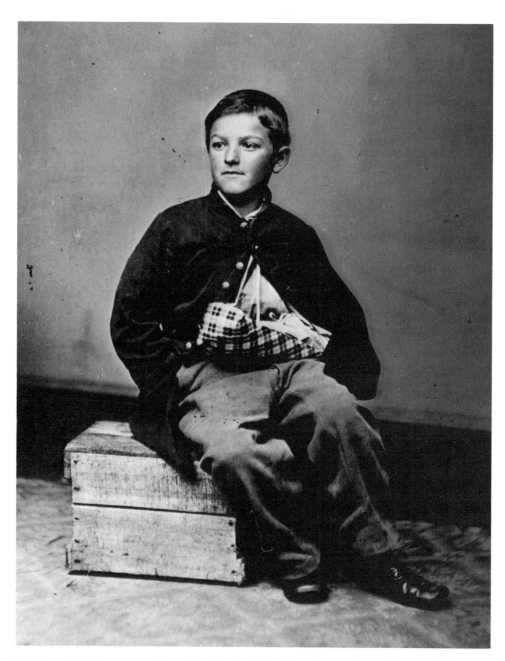

William Black was twelve when his left hand and arm were shattered by an exploding shell. He is considered the youngest wounded soldier of the war.

9

◇

"We're Going Home"

BY LATE 1864, MOST of the giant battles of the Civil War had been
fought, their names sounding like so many thudding cannon
booms—Shiloh, Antietam, Chancellorsville, Vicksburg, Gettysburg.
Each took a fearsome toll in lives; each brought the war a step closer to a
resolution. Now, Sherman was driving his army deep into the South,
splitting what was left of the Confederate army and leveling cities and
villages in his path. The war dragged along until April of the following
year, when the commander of the Confederate army, General Robert E.
Lee, officially surrendered at Appomattox.

Elisha Stockwell and his company were marching toward Montgom-
ery, Alabama, when "we got news that General Lee had surrendered,
and we lay there all day and celebrated. They lined up the artillery of the
whole command and fired a gun just about as fast as one could count.
An officer sat on a horse at the right of the gun, and he had a small flag
called a guidon. Every time he made a motion down a gun was fired. So
the firing was as regular as a clock. This sounded nice to us as it was the

death knell of secession and meant the cruel war was over." The next day, Stockwell and a friend gathered up their belongings and began walking home.

The ringing of bells and the firing of cannons announced the successful end of the Civil War to Northern troops and civilians. But many soldiers, especially those fighting for the Confederacy, learned by simple word of mouth. "We started back," one Southern boy wrote, "and it was not long before we began meeting soldiers from Lee's army. These men stated that Lee had surrendered. At first we thought them deserters. We pushed forward. The faster we marched the faster these soldiers came, until at last the courier met a man he knew; this man confirmed the report of Lee's surrender. I turned to the courier and asked: 'What are you going to do?' He answered, 'I'm going home.' I then said, 'I am going with you.' He did not object."

As both Stockwell and this Southern boy show, soldiers still possessed a remarkable degree of independence. They had signed on to fight until the war was over. Now that it was, the army could not tell them what to do. Thousands of soldiers from both armies simply left camp without waiting to be officially dismissed from duty. Southern soldiers had another reason for taking off so quickly. If they could avoid being captured and forced to surrender their weapons, they would strike a small, personal victory for their side.

The reception these boys received at home varied, of course. A grand review was held in Washington, D.C., for those Union soldiers who had not wandered off. Two hundred thousand marched up Pennsylvania Avenue and past the president, his cabinet, and tens of thousands of cheering citizens.

"They were proud of their achievements," an officer remarked, "and had the swing of men who had marched through half a dozen states." Needless to say, this wasn't a typical military parade, as the officer notes:

The Union Army parading up Washington's Pennsylvania Avenue in a final Grand Review, 1865.

"The feature of the column which seemed to interest the spectators most was the attachments of foragers in the rear of each brigade. [These] men appeared 'in their native ugliness' as they appeared on the march through Georgia and the Carolinas. Their pack mules and horses, with rope bridles or halters, laden with supplies. . . . It was a new feature in a grand review, but one which those who witnessed it will never forget."

The reception given Union soldiers in their hometowns and villages would be smaller but no less spirited. The boys were not just heroes, they were walking miracles. They had fought and preserved the Union *and* they had survived a war that had killed and injured a frightening number of soldiers. This celebration of relief and praise would continue for several years, culminating in a gigantic Peace Jubilee in 1869. There a chorus of ten thousand singers and almost one thousand instruments welcomed the soldiers home with what had to be an overwhelming rendition of "When Johnny Comes Marching Home."

> When Johnny comes marching home again, hurrah, hurrah!
> We'll give him a hearty welcome then, hurrah, hurrah!
> The men will cheer, the boys will shout,
> The ladies they will all turn out,
> And we'll all feel gay when Johnny comes marching home.
> And we'll all feel gay when Johnny comes marching home.

Confederate soldiers returned to a somewhat more subdued welcome. The South had lost the war, of course, but most soldiers did not feel defeated. For four years, they had held off an enemy that had had more money, men, and supplies than their side, and they had inflicted severe punishment on them, too. Most felt that if a few things had gone in their favor, they could have carried the fighting on longer and defeated the North.

This feeling grew into a passionate belief as time went on; regiments of Southern soldiers would meet for years to follow to debate what had happened and why. Adding fuel to this was a simmering anger that few tried to conceal. "8:30. We are moving briskly towards Richmond," John Delhaney would write, "and about 12 in the day I step off the train and proceed up the street. I shall not attempt to describe my feelings. The city in ruins and the hated and triumphant army of our malignant foes marching through the ruined city. With a raging headache and a swelling heart I reach my home, and here the curtain falls."

But the most common reaction must have been one of shock—at the changes the war brought to their society, the landscape, and themselves. One Confederate boy struggled for several days to get home, avoiding Union soldiers and eating what he could find along the way. Then, he writes, "I reached home May 25th, 1865. I found my father and mother working in the garden. Neither knew me at first glance, but when I smiled and spoke to them, mother recognized me and with tears of joy clasped me to her arms. My father stood by gazing upon me in mute admiration. Their long-lost boy had been found."

The ruins of Richmond, Virginia, as they appeared in April 1865.

Afterword
Acknowledgments and Sources
Select Bibliography
Index

Afterword

The war was over. Soon the homecoming celebrations, parades, and cemetery dedications were over, too, and the nation began trying to sort out what had just taken place. The result was a barrage of books written by politicians, soldiers, and historians from both sides. A curious thing happened during the writing of these various histories: The role played by boys in the war seemed to have been forgotten.

The War Department tacitly acknowledged the extent to which boys had taken part in the war. They effected a series of procedure changes that made it almost impossible for an underaged boy to enlist in the army, even in the supposedly "non-combat" positions of musician and telegraph operator. This meant that the Civil War was the last time large numbers of boys were able to fight for the United States.

Some boys did write about their experiences, but most of these writings were published privately and never received the acclaim given to books written by older men. Not until fairly recently did historians take a serious look at who had participated in the war and realize how many boys had managed to enlist. This shouldn't have surprised them, however. Boys have always been among the first to volunteer to fight. It happened during our own Revolutionary War, and it is still happening today in places like China, Latin America, South Africa, and the Mideast. Initially, boys might join the army to find adventure, to escape boredom, or to be where their friends are. But in the end, they fight and die for the same reason as older soldiers—to defend their homes and their freedom.

Acknowledgments and Sources

I want to thank the following individuals and institutions for their ideas, encouragement, and help in locating research materials and photographs: Philip Gibson, Photographic Services, the American Red Cross; Ann Salter, Archivist, Atlanta Historical Society; The Connecticut State Library; Dr. Mattie U. Russell, Curator of Manuscripts, Duke University; Jerry L. Kearns, The Library of Congress; The Mississippi Department of Archives and History; Barbara Burger, Archivist, The National Archives and Records Service; The New-York Historical Society; Daniel E. O'Brien, Curator, Ordnance Museum, the United States Army; Kermit J. Pike, Librarian, Western Reserve Historical Society; James C. Giblin; Eileen Mullen; and The Smithsonian Institution.

The following libraries were especially rich sources of autobiographies, diaries, memoirs, and collected letters of Civil War soldiers, as well as their regimental histories: The East Orange Public Library, The Newark Public Library, and The New York Public Library.

Select Bibliography

There have been more than fifty thousand books written about the Civil War—more than for any other war involving the United States. What follows is a very select list of some of the more interesting titles.

Abernethy, Byron R., ed. *Private Elisha Stockwell, Jr. Sees the Civil War.* Norman, OK, 1958.

Adams, George Worthington. *Doctors in Blue: The Medical History of the Union Army in the Civil War.* New York, 1952.

Ambrose, Stephen E., ed. *A Wisconsin Boy In Dixie: The Selected Letters of James K. Newton.* Madison, WI, 1961.

Bailey, George W. *A Private Chapter of the War (1861–1865).* St. Louis, 1880.

Billings, John D. *Hardtack and Coffee, or, The Unwritten Story of Army Life.* Boston, 1887.

Boney, F. N. *A Union Soldier in the Land of the Vanquished: The Diary of Sergeant Mathew Woodruff, June–December, 1865.* University of Alabama, 1969.

Brooks, U. R. *Butler and His Cavalry in the War of Secession 1861–1865.* Columbia, SC, 1909.

Catton, Bruce. *Glory Road: The Bloody Route from Fredericksburg to Gettysburg.* New York, 1952.

_____. *The Civil War.* New York, 1985.

_____. *This Hallowed Ground: The Story of the Union Side of the Civil War.* Garden City, NY, 1956.

Century Magazine, ed. *The Century War Book: The Famous History of the Civil War by the People Who Actually Fought It.* New York, 1894.

Commager, Henry Steele, ed. *The Blue and the Gray: The Story of the Civil War as Told by Participants: Volume One: The Nomination of Lincoln to the Eve of Gettysburg.* Indianapolis, 1950.

_____. *The Blue and the Gray: The Story of the Civil War as Told by Participants: Volume Two: The Battle of Gettysburg to Appomattox.* Indianapolis, 1950.

Davis, Burke. *The Civil War: Strange & Fascinating Facts.* New York, 1982.

Davis, William C., ed. *The Image of War 1861–1865,* 6 vols. Garden City, NY, 1981–1984.

Donald, David Herbert, ed. *Gone for a Soldier: The Civil War Memoirs of Private Alfred Bellard.* Boston, 1975.

Doubleday, Abner. *Reminiscences of Forts Sumter and Moultrie, 1860–1861.* New York, 1876.

Dowdey, Clifford. *The Land They Fought For: The Story of the South as the Confederacy, 1832–1865.* Garden City, NY, 1955.

Durkin, Joseph T., ed. *Confederate Chaplain: A War Journal of Rev. James B. Sheeran, C.Ss. R., 14th Louisiana, C.S.A.* Milwaukee, 1960.

Fatout, Paul. *Letters of a Civil War Surgeon.* Purdue Universities, 1961.

Foote, Shelby. *The Civil War: A Narrative,* 3 vols. New York, 1958–1974.

Galway, Thomas Francis. *The Valiant Hours.* Harrisburg, PA, 1946.

Goss, Warren Lee. *Recollections of a Private: A Story of the Army of the Potomac.* New York, 1890.

Halsey, Ashley, ed. *A Yankee Private's Civil War by Robert Hale Strong.* Chicago, 1961.

Hesseltine, William B. *Civil War Prisons: A Study in War Psychology.* Columbus, OH, 1930.

Jackson, Joseph Orville, ed. *"Some of the Boys. . . .": The Civil War Letters of Isaac Jackson, 1862–1865.* Carbondale, IL, 1960.

Long, E. B. *The Civil War Day by Day: An Almanac, 1861–1865.* New York, 1971.

McCarthy, Carlton. *Detailed Minutiae of Soldier Life in the Army of Northern Virginia, 1861–1865.* Richmond, VA, 1882.

McPherson, James M. *Battle Cry of Freedom: The Civil War Era.* New York, 1988.

Miller, Francis T., ed. *The Photographic History of the Civil War,* 10 vols. New York, 1911.

Mitchell, Reid. *Civil War Soldiers: Their Expectations and Their Experiences.* New York, 1988.

Nott, Charles C. *Sketches of the War: A Series of Letters to the North Moore Street School.* New York, 1865.

Silver, James W., ed. *A Life for the Confederacy: As Recorded in the Pocket Diaries of Pvt. Robert A. Moore.* Jackson, TN, 1959.

Truxall, Aida Craig, ed. *"Respects to All": Letters of Two Pennsylvania Boys in the War of Rebellion.* Pittsburgh, 1961.

Walton, Clyde C., ed. *Private Smith's Journal: Recollections of the Late War.* Chicago, 1963.

Wiley, Bell I. *The Life of Johnny Reb: The Common Soldier of the Confederacy.* Indianapolis, 1943.

_____. *The Life of Billy Yank: The Common Soldier of the Union.* Baton Rouge, LA, 1983.

Willis, Charles W. *Army Life of an Illinois Soldier.* Washington, 1906.

Winther, Oscar Osburn, ed. *With Sherman to the Sea: Journal of Theodore Upson.* Baton Rouge, LA, 1943.

Winthrop, Theodore. *Life in the Open Air, and Other Papers.* Boston, 1863.

Index